First Edition
Genuine Autographed Collectible

Do you want me to sign it in ink or in lipstick?

Tohu Vavohu
Simchat Torah: Genesis 1.2

Gift Card

Date:

To:

From:

Message:

Tohu Vavohu: Chaos, Confusion, or Disorder

Tohu Vavohu is a Biblical Hebrew phrase that describes the state of the earth before the creation of light. It is made up of two words, tohu, which means "formlessness" or "confusion," and vavohu, which means "emptiness." The phrase is often used to describe a state of chaos, confusion, or disorder. We read this on the holiday of SIMCHAT TORAH — the day of the Oct 7TH genocide.

Q: Why did Oct 7TH occur on the happiest Jewish holiday of Simchat Torah?

This Is the Spiritual Challenge: Bring More Light into the World

Instead of drowning in your pain, you have to force yourself to celebrate Simchat Torah. The holiday is the spiritual force that prevents you from succumbing to your wounds. You must embrace life, and move forward into the next year.

Israel brought more **LIGHT** into the **WORLD** by defeating two terrorist armies: HAMAS and HEZBOLLAH. In two weeks, the Syrian axis of evil fell.

Prime Minister Golda Meir said that after every war, Israel expands her territory reclaiming her ancestral homeland.

And God said, "Let there be light," and there was light.

Sharon Esther Lampert
PRINCESS KADIMAH
8TH PROPHETESS OF ISRAEL
GOD IS GO! DO!
THE 22 COMMANDMENTS

Tohu Vavohu
Simchat Torah: Genesis 1.2
October 7, 2023

Genesis 1.2 Now the Earth was Formless and Empty, Darkness was Over the Surface of the Deep, and the Spirit of God was Hovering over the Waters

GENESIS 1.2 (MT)
WORDS 1 - 7

פני	על	וחשך	ובהו	תהו	היתה	והארץ
the surface	was over	darkness	empty and	formless	was	earth the Now
140	100	334	19	411	420	302

Sum = 1726

Biblical Prophecy

HAMAS = VIOLENCE

Did you know that the Bible speaks about **"Hamas?"**

Not only once, or twice; but you can find hamas mentioned **60 times** in the Old Testament.

Example 1.
"And God said unto Noah, the end of all flesh is come before me; for the earth is filled with **violence** through them; and, behold, I will destroy them with the earth" (Gen. 6:13).

Example 2.
"O Lord, how long shall I cry, and You will not hear? Even cry out to You, **'Violence!'** and You will not save?" (Habakkuk 1:2).

Each of those passages mentions hamas; but you would only see it if you were looking at the passage in its original Hebrew language.

In the above passages the word translated as **"violence"** comes from the Hebrew word, **"Hamas";** and though commonly interpreted as **"violence,"** it actually connotes any type of unjust destructive, harmful and life-denying behavior.

You Cannot Negotiate with Evil
Destroy the Evil or Be Destroyed by the Evil

Education Cannot Ameliorate Anti-Semitism
Haters Hate the Truth, the Facts, and the Light

Israel Has All the Right Friends and All the Right Enemies!

KING BIBI Is the Greatest World Leader Since the Dawn of History!

Sharon Esther Lampert
Princess Kadimah 8TH Prophetess of Israel
GOD IS GO! DO!
THE 22 COMMANDMENTS

Jewish History, Judaism, October 7, 2023, Sharon Esther Lampert

TOHU VAVOHU - SIMCHAT TORAH - October 7TH, 2023

©2024 First Edition by Sharon Esther Lampert. All Rights Reserved.

No part of this book may be used or reproduced in any manner whatsoever without written permission except in the case of brief quotations embodied in critical articles and reviews.
No part of this book may be used or reproduced in any manner for the purpose of training artificial intelligence technologies or systems. In accordance with Article 4(3) of the Digital Single Market Directive 2019/790, (KADIMAH PRESS) expressly reserves this work from the text and data mining exception.

KADIMAH PRESS
GIFTS OF GENIUS

Books may be purchased for education, business, or sales promotional use.
ISBN Hardcover: 979-8-3305-9161-9
ISBN Paperback: 979-8-3305-9176-3
ISBN E-Book: 979-8-3305-9177-0
Library of Congress Catalog Card Number: 2024924842

FAN MAIL:
SharonEstherLampert.com
FANS@SharonEstherLampert.com

Cover and Interior Book Design: Creative Genius Sharon Esther Lampert

Editor: Dave Segal
Palm Beach Book Publisher, Phone: 917-767-5843
Sharon@PalmBeachBookPublisher.com

To Order Book:
Ingram, 1 Ingram Blvd. La Vergne, TN 37086-3629
Phone: 615-793-5000
Fax orders: 615-287-6990

First Edition

Manufactured in the United States of America

Age 9
THE QUEEN HAS ARRIVED!
My daughter is a poet, philosopher, and teacher. She is the Princess & Pea!
BEAUTY & BRAINS!
LOVE & XOXO
MOMMY

What Do Books Do?
BOOKS ARE POWERFUL

Books Educate!
Books Enlighten!
Books Empower!
Books Emancipate!
Books Entertain!
Books Spring Eternal!
Books Drive Exploration!
Books Spark Evolution!
Books Ignite Revolution!

Sharon Esther Lampert

In Memory of Innocent Lives Lost
May Their Memories Be a Blessing

Jews, Christians, Hindus, Buddhists, Muslims, Druzes, Bedouins

Hashem Yinkom Domon - May God Avenge Their Blood

Baruch Da'ayan Ha'amet - Blessed Be the Judge Who Judges the Truth

NETZACH YISRAEL LO YISHAKER — THE JEWISH PEOPLE ARE ETERNAL

SAMUEL I 15:29

Tohu Vavohu

Simchat Torah: Genesis 1.2
October 7, 2023

Genesis 1.2 Now the Earth was Formless and Empty, Darkness was Over the Surface of the Deep, and the Spirit of God was Hovering over the Waters

6:37 a.m.

I hear wolves howling:

"Allalu Akbar!"
"Allalu Akbar!"
"Allalu Akbar!"
"Allalu Akbar!"
"Allalu Akbar!"
"Allalu Akbar!"
"Allalu Akbar!"
"Allalu Akbar!"

Operation Al-Aqsa Flood

Outside gunfire yowls:
I see green headbands,
AK-47s, and motorcycles
in my window

"Allalu Akbar!"
"Allalu Akbar!"
"Allalu Akbar!"

Re'im Music Festival Massacre

Be'eri massacre

Kissufim massacre

Ein HaShlosha massacre

Nahal Oz massacre

I text loved ones: "Terrorists!"

Nir Oz massacre

Kfar Aza massacre

Battle of Sderot

Netiv HaAsara massacre

Holit massacre

Nirim massacre

Yakhini massacre

Alumim massacre

I hear thousands of rockets booming...
BOOM! BOOM! BOOM! BOOM! BOOM!
BOOM! BOOM! BOOM! BOOM! BOOM!
BOOM! BOOM! BOOM! BOOM! BOOM!
BOOM! BOOM! BOOM! BOOM! BOOM!
BOOM! BOOM! BOOM! BOOM! BOOM!
BOOM! BOOM! BOOM! BOOM! BOOM!
BOOM! BOOM! BOOM! BOOM! BOOM!
BOOM! BOOM! BOOM! BOOM! BOOM!
BOOM! BOOM! BOOM! BOOM! BOOM!
BOOM! BOOM! BOOM! BOOM! BOOM!
BOOM! BOOM! BOOM! BOOM! BOOM!

I run to the bomb shelter:
Barefoot in pajamas
Forgot water
Forgot snacks
Forgot cell phone charger
No weapon
Shelter door doesn't lock
- Tohu Vavohu -

"Allalu Akbar!"
"Allalu Akbar!"
"Allalu Akbar!"

Re'im Music Festival Massacre   **Be'eri massacre**   **Kissufim massacre**

Ein HaShlosha massacre   **Nahal Oz massacre**

I send a final text: "I Love You!"

Nir Oz massacre   **Kfar Aza massacre**

Battle of Sderot   **Netiv HaAsara massacre**   **Holit massacre**

Nirim massacre   **Yakhini massacre**   **Alumim massacre**

Hamas terrorists are in my house
Palestinian civilians are in my house
Raided refrigerator: stole cans of whipped cream!
Looted home
Graffitied walls

"Allalu Akbar!"
"Allalu Akbar!"
"Allalu Akbar!"

"Allalu Akbar!"
"Allalu Akbar!"
"Allalu Akbar!"

My loved ones murdered in
front of my own eyes
Stabbed pregnant daughter in stomach
Beheaded one grandson
Raped one granddaughter
Family dog is shot dead
Ashes remain of whole families burned alive
Hamas posted murders on my Facebook page
Used my cell phone and their GO PRO cameras
Hamas cuts electricity to Kibbutz

"Allalu Akbar!"
"Allalu Akbar!"
"Allalu Akbar!"

"Allalu Akbar!"
"Allalu Akbar!"
"Allalu Akbar!"

My house is set on fire
My family is set on fire
My fields are set on fire
My car is set on fire
GENOCIDE!

"Allalu Akbar!"
"Allalu Akbar!"
"Allalu Akbar!"

Hamas Abduction of Grandma

Tossed me on a motorcycle barefoot in pajamas

Hit me with sticks
Lost my eye glasses
Stole my wedding band
Ripped my necklace off my neck
Pulled my earrings out of my ears
Ripped my watch off my wrist
Drove me to GAZA in my own car
Last cell phone signal is in GAZA

– Tohu Vavohu –

"Allalu Akbar!"
"Allalu Akbar!"
"Allalu Akbar!"

"Allalu Akbar!"
"Allalu Akbar!"
"Allalu Akbar!"

Hamas Captivity

Walked miles barefoot through murky underground tunnels
Sat in a pitch black tunnel for weeks
Slept on a dirty floor mattress
Breathed in filthy air
Ate a daily slice of pita – sipped dirty water
Thai hostage ate toilet paper
Tortured & raped hostages
Learned 250 words in Arabic
No medications
No hearing aids
No Red Cross
50 days in captivity
50 days no shower
No soap – skin disease
Buried alive in a hijab
Buried alive in an underground cage
Moved us around to 10 different locations
Made a viral hostage propaganda video
Don't let us cry! Don't let us talk! We whisper!

-Tohu Vavohu -

"Allalu Akbar!"
"Allalu Akbar!"
"Allalu Akbar!"

Hamas Abduction of 251 Hostages

Dead Shani Louk paraded in GAZA –

wins photo of the year contest!

Dead Israeli soldiers are taken hostage

Beheaded soldier's head is taken hostage

"Allalu Akbar!"
"Allalu Akbar!"
"Allalu Akbar!"

The whole Bibas family is taken hostage

Hamas Executes Hostages in Captivity

Palestinian civilians hit hostages upon arrival
Palestinian civilians celebrate with candy
-Tohu Vavohu -

HAMAS IS ISIS

Maim one
Mutilate one
Murder one
Rape one
Behead one
Take one hostage!
Burn babies alive!

Terrorist texts photos of murdered loved ones on Facebook
Terrorist calls his mother to brag about murdering 10 Jews

— Tohu Vavohu —

Hamas Chit-Chat with Hostages

"It's fine. Your murdered daughter is with Allah"

"I'm sorry! — It is against the Quran"

"Move to Tel Aviv... We will be back!"

"Israel is no more... You will live in Gaza forever!

"You will convert to Islam, marry me, and have my baby!"

— Tohu Vavohu —

"Allalu Akbar!"
"Allalu Akbar!"
"Allalu Akbar!"

"Allalu Akbar!"
"Allalu Akbar!"
"Allalu Akbar!"

18 Hours In a Bomb Shelter

No water

No food

No bathroom

No cell phone battery

No cell phone charger

No cell phone service

No Israeli police

No Israeli army

"Allalu Akbar!"
"Allalu Akbar!"
"Allalu Akbar"

Israeli border guards slaughtered

Israeli police force slaughtered

399 Nova Dance Festival of Peace victims raped and slaughtered

1200 Jews Murdered In Their Homeland Tohu Vavohu!

Never Again Is Now!

7 Front War

IRANIAN RING OF FIRE

Rockets from Gaza

Rockets from Lebanon

Rockets from Yemen

Rockets from Syria

Rockets from Iraq

— Tohu Vavohu —

"Allalu Akbar!"
"Allalu Akbar!"
"Allalu Akbar!"

Ballistic Missiles from Iran
Terrorist Attacks from West Bank

Ten Million Israelis Run to Bomb Shelters

Hostage Exchanges
Prisoners Are Released from Prison
— Only in the West Bank —
Arabs Rejoice that Criminals Are Released Back into the Neighborhood
— Tohu Vavohu —

"Allalu Akbar!"   "Allalu Akbar!"
"Allalu Akbar!"   "Allalu Akbar!"
"Allalu Akbar!"   "Allalu Akbar!"

I am one of the lucky ones: **ALIVE!**

I have to smile and wave goodbye to Hamas terrorists for the TV cameras!

Loving embrace by State of Israel: **AMEN!**

In the hospital, therapy dogs shower me with wet kisses! **A Mechayeh!**

Horrible photo of **ME** on a hostage poster plastered worldwide: **Oy Vey!**

I lost lots of weight! My hair is full of lice! My hijab has blood stains!

I am covered in bruises — terror, nightmares, trauma — PTSD for Life!

My husband is still in GAZA — so a piece of my heart is still in GAZA

Daughter and son-in-law murdered - no time to grieve and mourn!

Orphaned during the Holocaust — I raise my orphaned grandchildren

Neighbors burned alive — funerals without bodies

Everyone knows somebody who lost a loved one

After 40 years of beautiful memories living in my kibbutz, I am homeless in my own homeland

Tohu Vavohu!

Centuries of Islamic Jihadist Holy Wars and Sharia Law in The Name of Allah

Tohu Vavohu!

"HAIL TO JIHAD"

Jews Santify Life
Jihadists Glorify Death

Arabs Learned Nothing from 1948, 1967, and 1973
Israel Is an Eagle in the Sky
Arabs Are Underground Rats

Arabs Do Not **CALCULATE** Their Own Defeat By The **GOD OF ISRAEL**

Al-Aqsa Mosque Drives Them Mad!

HAMAS CHARTER

The Covenant of the Islamic Resistance Movement was Issued on August 18, 1988

"Israel will exist and will continue to exist until **ISLAM** will obliterate it, just as it obliterated others before it."

Tohu Vavohu!
FLEE to FREE
SYSTEM FAILURE

In Every War, Civilians Flee to Neighboring Countries!
Arabs in West Bank & Gaza Cannot FLEE to FREE!
There Are 21 Arab Countries and 57 Muslim Countries

Prime Minister Golda Meir said:
"In every war the Arabs start,
Arabs lose their territory, and return
to Israel her ancestral homeland."

Genesis 1.3 God said, "Let There Be Light!"

Tohu Vavohu!

UNITED NATIONS
SYSTEM FAILURE

UNRWA
75 Years of Refugees

UN SCHOOLS
Terrorist Infrastructure

UN Employees
Terrorists

UN Failure to Condemn RAPE

RED CROSS SYSTEM FAILURE

WORLD FOOD KITCHEN SYSTEM FAILURE

Files Resolutions That Do Not Condemn Hamas or Release the 101 Hostages

UN Peacekeepers in Lebanon Fail to Implement 1701

"Conquer the Galilee"

— Diplomatic Terrorism —

Tohu Vavohu!
INTERNATIONAL CRIMINAL COURT SYSTEM FAILURE

AMNESTY INTERNATIONAL SYSTEM FAILURE

Files an Arrest Warrent for a Dead Terrorist

Files an Arrest Warrent for KING BIBI The Greatest World Leader Since the Dawn of History!

900,000 Tons of Food in Gaza ICC Files a Charge of "Starvation"

— Diplomatic Terrorism —

Tohu Vavohu!
MEDIA SYSTEM FAILURE

- Failure to Fact Check -

Hamas Combatants vs. Gaza Civilians
Rapes Never Happened
Babies Never Murdered
No Food into Gaza
Interviews with "Iranian Useful Idiots" - Bassam Comedian

No Media Reports on Terrorist Cells on Public City Streets Waving Terrorist Flags

Tohu Vavohu!
College Presidents and Encampments
THE KNOW NOTHINGS!
— Iranian Useful Idiots —

"Calling for the Genocide of Jews Is a Matter of Context!"

Ivy League Presidents Are Fired or Resign
Harvard, Columbia, Upenn, and Cornell
Flunked Moral Clarity or Moral Rot Test!
Students Are Arrested & Suspended
Flunked History!

Tohu Vavohu!

BERNIE SANDERS
SYSTEM FAILURE
"Iranian Useful Idiot"

Files a Resolution to Block Aid to Israel

Hamas Murdered 43 Americans

Hamas Takes 12 Americans Hostage

7 Americans Still in Captivity

Bernie Sanders Can't NAME Any of Them!

Edan Alexander, Itay Chen, Sagui Dekel-Chen, Gad Haggai, Judi Weinstein, Omer Neutra, and Keith Siegal

Tohu Vavohu!

Global Intifada
Dar-Al-Harb: House of War

Spreading Lies
"Israel is Killing Babies and Children!"
Indoctrinarion of Hatred
and
Assaults on Jewish Communities in Cities:

New York, London, Berlin, Montreal, Dublin
Amsterdam, and Dubai Rabbi Zvi Kogen

Tohu Vavohu!
Hamas Hostage Strategy

HAMAS Sacrifices Two Million Gazans and Refuses to Release Israeli Hostages to Keep the War Going ... So That

HEZBOLLAH, IRAN, and HOUTHIS will Destroy Israel — and to

Incite a **GLOBAL INTIFADA**
The War Against All Jews

Israeli Hostages Are Hamas Human Shields Against Israeli Aggression in Gaza

5-Million Dollar Reward May Help Keep Hostages from Execution

Tohu Vavohu
Worst Case Scenario

1. 21 Arab Countries Refuse to Absorb Gazan Refugees

2. No One Wants to PAY to Rebuild Gaza

3. Gazans Live in Tents for Generations Surviving on Foreign Aid

4. The IDF Retrieves the Bodies of Hostages One-by-One for the Next Ten Years!

5. Some Hostages Are Lost and Never Return Home for Burial

6. Hamas Executes All Hostages

PAY FOR SLAY

Tohu Vavohu!
Tragedy, Trials, and Trauma

For 36 YEARS
HAMAS Murdered Innocent Civilians of All Nationalities and Faiths

For 18 YEARS
HAMAS Turned GAZA into an Underground Fortress to Launch Rockets into Israel

For Centuries ...
Holy Wars Against the Infidels in the Name of Allah
"Allalu Akbar!"

Tohu Vavohu!
Oct 7 Celebrations

Q: Where Are the Protestors for Hamas to Surrender and Release the Hostages? NONE! Protestors Rip Down Hostage Posters!

Q: Where Are the Protestors for Hamas to Stop Shooting at Palestinians who Follow Israeli Evacuation Orders?

Q: Where Are the Protestors for Hamas to Stop Stealing Palestinian Foreign Food Aid?

All Protests Call for a Global Intifada Against Jews! Protestors Celebrate the Oct 7TH Massacre

Tohu Vavohu!
75 Years of Refugees

**The Country of Palestine Never Existed
Palestine Was a British Territory**

**Palestinian Arabs Live in Jordan, Lebanon, Syria,
and in Judea and Sameria**

**UN Status as Arab Refugees for 75 Years
UN EDUCATION SYSTEM FAILURE**

**For 75 Years, Failed at Building a Civilized Society
No Leadership! No Moral Compass!**

**Transformed GAZA into an Underground Fortress
to Launch Rockets into Israel
Billions of International Dollars Squandered**

Tohu Vavohu! Trauma & Trap

ISRAEL
Is at the Forefront of Science, Technology, Medicine, and Ai
Israel Has 13 Noble Prizes
ISRAELIS Do Not Have Time to Dismantle Terrorist Infrastructure and Neutralize Terrorists and Argue with the Know Nothings!

Tohu Vavohu!
Palestinian State Erase & Replace

Not Even ONE Palestinian Is Protesting for a Two-State Solution Every Protester Is Calling for the Destruction of the State of Israel, For a Global Intifada Against Jews, and For an ISLAMIC HOLY WAR, a Muslim Caliphate, and Sharia Law "Allalu Akbar!"

Tohu Vavohu! WITCH HUNT

KING BIBI
Prime Minister Benjaimin Netanyahu
The Greatest World Leader Since the Dawn of History!
16 Years+ - 24/7 Dedication

Case 1000: Gifts for Favors
Case 2000: Legislative Deals
Case 4000: Telecommunications Deals

There Is a 9 Front War ...
This Can Wait!

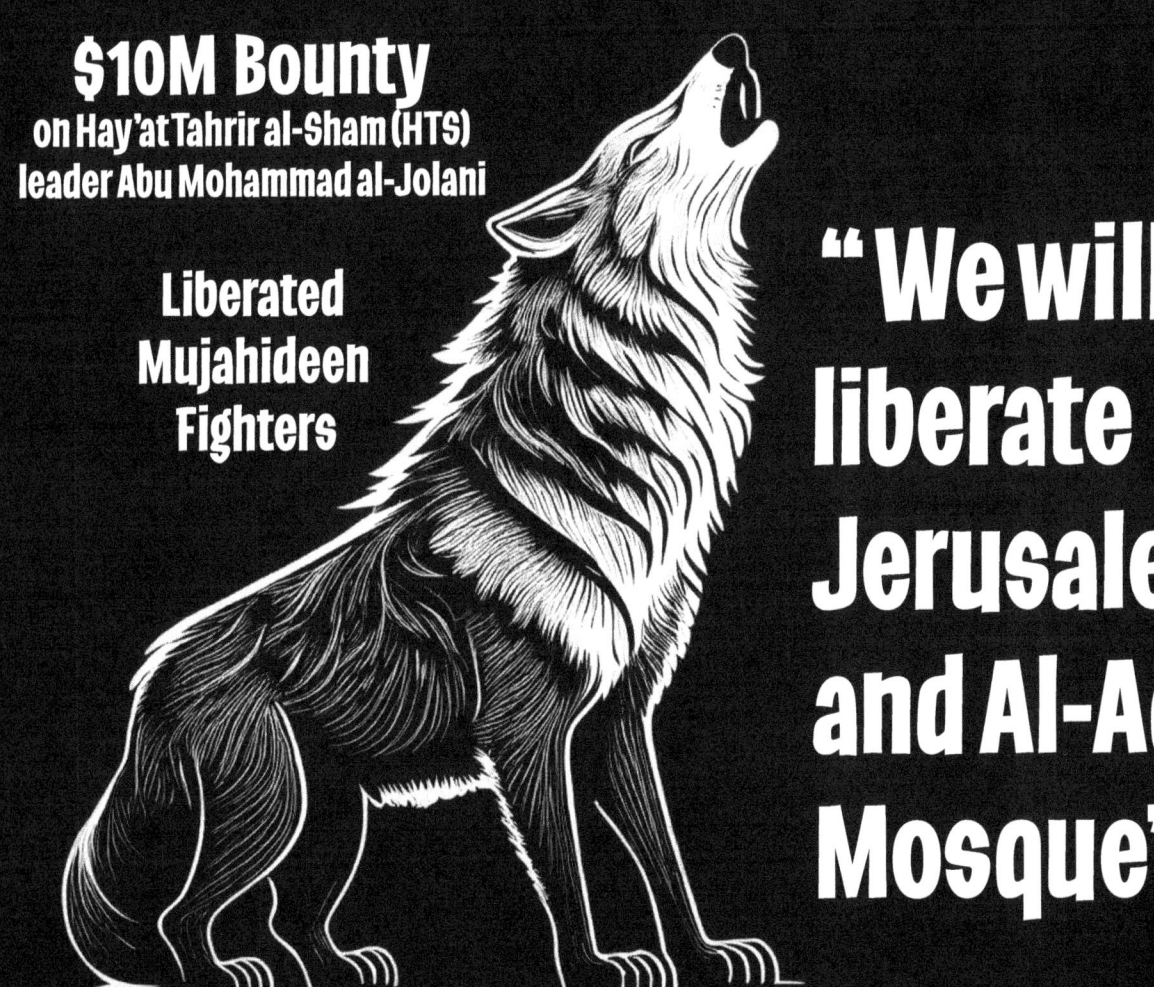

Tohu Vavohu!
Terrorist Organizations Hijacked Entire Countries

FREE Gaza from Hamas ISIS
FREE West Bank from Hamas ISIS
FREE Lebanon from Hezbollah
FREE Yemen from Houthis
FREE Iran from Iranian Republic
FREE Syria from ISIS, Al-Qaeda
FREE Iraq from Iranian Republic
FREE Afghanistan from Taliban

I hear wolves howling:
"Allalu Akbar!"
"Allalu Akbar!"
"Allalu Akbar!"
"Allalu Akbar!"
"Allalu Akbar!"
"Allalu Akbar!"
"Allalu Akbar!"
"Allalu Akbar!"

Jihadist Terrorist Cells Infiltrate the Democratic Free World

FREE Europe from Terrorist Cells   "Death to Germany!"
FREE America from Terrorist Cells   "Death to America!"
FREE Canada from Terrorist Cells   "Death to Canada!"
FREE Australia from Terrorist Cells "Death to Australia!"

Hungary and Poland get the ... last laugh... by refusing to let Muslim refugees into their countries!

I have always enjoyed baking cookies for my grandchildren. This year on the Jewish holiday of Purim, I will bake:

HAMENtashen
HAMAStashen
HEZBOLtashen
HOUTHItashen
HEADofSNAKEtashen
AM YISRAEL CHAI

Released Grandma Hostages:
Grandma Yafa Adar, Age 85
Grandma Yocheved Lifshitz, Age 85
Grandma Ditza Heiman, Age 84
Grandma Nurit Cooper, Age 79
Grandma Hannah Perry, Age 79
Grandma Tamar Metzger, Age 78
Grandma Ruthi Monder, Age 78
Grandma Ofelia Roitman, Age 77
Grandmother Hanna Katzir, Age 77
Grandma Margalit Mozes, Age 77
Grabdma Ada Sagi, Age 75
Grandma Adina Moshe, Age 72
Grandma Shoshan Haran, Age 67
Grandma Clara Merman, Age 63
Grandma Aviva Adrian Siegel, Age 62

Grandma Judi Weinstein Haggai, Age 70
Grandma Ofra Keidar, Age 70
Hostages in Gaza
Murdered by Hamas in Captivity
May God Avenge Their Blood!

GENESIS 1.3-4

3. And God said, "Let there be light," and there was light.

4. God saw that the light was good, and he separated the light from the darkness.

NEVER AGAIN! 1945
NEVER AGAIN IS NOW! OCT 7TH
NEVER FORGIVE! NEVER FORGET!
NOW OR NEVER! IRAN!

USA President Biden wants to **DEFEND** against terrorism but does not want to **DEFEAT** terrorism

USA President Bush wanted to **DEFEAT** terrorism
He played **OFFENSE** not **DEFENSE**!
DEFEAT Terrorists on Their Turf:

Iraq and Afghanistan (20 Years, Taliban Disaster)
10 Years to Neutralize Osama bin Laden in Pakistan

Progress = Paradigm Shifts

Get in Front of the Problem Before the Problem Gets in Front of You!

Priority 1. Trump Administration: Destroy Iranian Republic Nuclear Threat

Priority 2. Play Offense Not Defense - Destroy the Terrorists on Their Turf!

Priority 3. No Terrorist Hate Groups Allowed to Exist in the State of Israel

Priority 4. Change the Law: Terrorists Do Not Go to Jail — They Are Neutralized! Dead Bodies Will Not Be Returned to Family Members

Priority 5. Change the Name of the WEST BANK to JUDEA & SAMARIA

Priority 6. Build a University Dedicated to Educating Arab Leaders Who Will Be in Charge of Governing the Arabs in Jewish Ancestral Lands Hold Conferences to Educate Arab Leaders in 21 Arab Countries

Priority 7. Rebuild the Al-Aqsa Mosque in an Arab Country, and Transfer the "Foundation Rock" -- Rebuild the Third Temple!

Priority 8. Take Control of All of the Arab Schools and Education System

Priority 9. Take Control of the Media Channels: Misinformation Overload

Priority 10. Integration: Build Temples and Churches Next to Mosques

PRINCESS KADIMAH: THE 8TH PROPHETESS OF ISRAEL

THE DELIVERERS

MOSES
THE PROMISED LAND

ISRAEL DEFENSE FORCES
VICTORIES OF JOSHUA

KING DAVID
CAPITAL OF JERUSALEM

KING SOLOMON
THE FIRST TEMPLE

THEODORE HERZL
ZIONISM

DAVID BEN-GURION
STATE OF ISRAEL

BENJAMIN NETANYAHU
INNOVATION NATION

JEWS: THE CHOSEN PEOPLE

God of Abraham, Issac, and Jacob,
Deliverance of Moses, Victories of Joshua,
Courage of David, Wisdom of Solomon,
Heroism of Esther, Light of Maccabees,
Blessings of Generations of Pious Rabbis,
Dream of Herzl, Leadership of Ben-Gurion,
Queen Fundraiser Golda Meir,
Reign of King Bibi, Valor of Yoav Gallant,
Prowess of Tomer Bar, and Bravery of
Mighty Israel Defense Forces

AM YISRAEL CHAI

Sharon Esther Lampert
PRINCESS KADIMAH
8TH Prophetess of Israel
GOD IS GO! DO!
THE 22 COMMANDMENTS
Israeli Operation Iron Pen

KADIMAH PRESS: GIFTS OF GENIUS

First Woman to Write a Book on 5000 Years of Jewish History Using 6 Poetric Refrains

"Many Jews Reclaimed God"

3 Editions:
ISBN Hardcover: 979-8-8690-79-27-5
ISBN Paperback: 979-8-8690-79-31-2
ISBN e-book: 979-8-8690-79-28-2
Library of Congress: 2024900329

KADIMAH PRESS: GIFTS OF GENIUS

POETRY JEW-ELS
The Greatest Poems Ever Written on Extraordinary Jewish World Events

3 Editions:
ISBN Hardcover: 978-1-885872-15-9
ISBN Paperback: 978-1-885872-16-6
ISBN e-book: 978-1-885872-17-3
Library of Congress: 2022912158

Published 80+ Books

GENIUS: THE GIFT OF DIVINE REVELATION

MY BOOKS WRITE THEMSELVES

I Am Mortal
MY BOOKS ARE IMMORTAL
Please Handle My Books Gently
My Books Are My Remains

This book was written and published in one day:

Part 1.   Birth of Idea: October 20, 2023
Part 2.   Format Book: November 14, 2024
Part 3.   Publish: November 14, 2024
Part 4.   Updated: December 13, 2024

Sharon Esther Lampert
SEE THE WORLD THROUGH THE EYES OF A CREATIVE GENIUS
Prodigy, Prophet, Philosopher, Poet, Peacemaker, Paladin of Education, Physicist, Princess

FANS@SharonEstherLampert.com

www.ingramcontent.com/pod-product-compliance
Lightning Source LLC
LaVergne TN
LVHW072115060526
838201LV00011B/241